P9-ELH-703

DATE DUE

DEMCO 38-296

FOR A MODEST GOD

ALSO BY ERIC ORMSBY

Coastlines
Bavarian Shrine and Other Poems

FOR A MODEST GOD

New and Selected Poems

ERIC ORMSBY

Grove Press *New York*

Published simultaneously in Canada
Printed in the United States of America

FIRST EDITION

Library of Congress Cataloging-in-Publication Data
Ormsby, Eric L. (Eric Linn), 1941–
For a modest God : new and selected poems / Eric Ormsby.—1st ed.
p.   cm.
ISBN 0-8021-1607-8
I. Title.
PS3565.R59F6   1997
811'.54—dc20   96-35472

Design by Laura Hammond Hough

Grove Press
841 Broadway
New York, NY 10003

10 9 8 7 6 5 4 3 2 1

For Irena

do stříbra jsem vyryl
SINE AMORE NIHIL
bez lásky není nic.

In silver I have incised this verse
SINE AMORE NIHIL
without love is nothingness.
—Jan Skácel, *Sonet jako talisman*

CONTENTS

[ix]

PART ONE
FOR A MODEST GOD:
NEW POEMS

QUARK FOG

Let matter take on the shape of elands,
the hieratic pongo, or the great
eager emptiness in the spaces of love.
I ponder the temporary desert
of my hand. Matter will not
chisel a voice from this
fog of quarks.

If merest fable drops into the fog,
articulated stars assert
eclosion of the gold-sewn chrysalids.
Early nouns bob in blunt fens.
Verbs browse electrically in mist,
particles gnarl the stems of bulrush copulae.
In a pristine caldera of consonants,
vowel-magma brims and
virginal horizons spike
cordilleras of speech.

Sweetheart,
let haggard worlds await
the proton's aboriginal decay:

our sun is uttering her saffron palatals.

I

Ô ressources infinies de l'épaisseur des choses, rendues par les ressources infinies de l'épaisseur sémantique des mots!

—Francis Ponge

GAZING AT WAVES

At Morbihan or Montauk or at Peggy's
Cove, or where the little drab corniche
south of Casablanca runs to sand,
wherever there's an ocean promontory,
people always look far out to sea
as though expecting some unheard-of
apparition to arise, beyond the waves
where the horizon glitters like an eye
peeping through a sleepy eyelid.
                                    Why
do they look so searchingly out there?
Do they think the sea can offer more
than corrugated combers or
that queasy smell of peaches that the shore
concocts from mussel shells and clumps of kelp?

Maybe there's satisfaction in the prompt
pinnacles of waves, their tasseling
symmetrical ascensions, and that sense
precision amid pandemonium
provides.

At other times, more rarely now perhaps,
some little shiver of acknowledgment
still finds us there
between the stately troughings and the
counterglides, the scattered plash
of droplets, with the keen gulls
mewing and the rocks
reflective of a light too old for us,
and this gives back our
littleness again, this restores
some sort of privileged insignificance;
or will the waves always appear mere
sequent arrival without consequence?

The spectacle is sovereign, yet intimate.
How soon the waters enter our
attention, follow us in sleep,
accompany the cadence of our minds,
seem punctual and seriatim, curled
in all the beauty of futility,
so promptly mortal as they gather in,
ascend and hover in the gusting air,
then amble over into hiddenness,
fold themselves in sand like drowsy claws
curved into the twilight of the nest.
Is it a consolation to be witnesses
of what so lucidly evades our gaze?
Is gazing a favor that gazed waves bestow?

WHAT IT IS LIKE TO BE A BAT

Night is algorithmic: dark,
Archimedean. Cosines of echo
structure the night. A peep
subtends from the slick
bodies of crickets. The gauzy
reverberations of moths are not
the curt returns from smokestack or from arch.

Night is a cloth, crinkling
with secret threads, alert
to the listening ear as any sun.
Night is a calculus
of cries where bodies are
connected in the parallax
of coincident voices, ripple-precise.

Night plinks with voices.
There are the torn orbits
of escaping voices, the stridulence
of beetles, steely timbres of the katydid.
There are loving collocations
of ridges known only by sound-shadows, loud
shards of home demarcated by pipings
in darkness beyond all superfluities
of sight. There are the welcoming crests
of other cries, sweeter than the green
panic of lacewings, that phosphor
all along the sleep-furred, down-
gloved bodies of our caverned families.

THE ANT LION

Beneath your shoe soles there's a beautiful
concavity of sand, a symmetrical
funnel the width of a small boy's thumb.
It looks expertly smooth. Precarious
sand grains have been set to slide
whenever a plodding ant's insouciance
pitches it down that soft declivity.
The owner of the pit abides down there,
a drab predator the color of
quarry rock, old spackle, gypsum, slate.
Earth-colored, with the shadows of the earth,
he snuggles in the hollow of his snare.

At night, in childhood, I would sometimes dream
of the panicky scrambles of a slipping ant,
its scurrying despair that swept it down
irresistibly along the volatile sand.
The way that dreams deceive you the ant fell
and I, asleep, felt falling too
through filmy floorboards into avalanche
as the heart-stopped terror of my helpless dream
tossed me to the soft mouth of the pit.
There, with upswung jaws, the ant lion
wiggled out of ambush, rushed to hug
me, his frantic victim, in a pinch. That
too had the horrible embrace of dream
where you choke those you love or they choke you
and everything takes place mechanically
despite the shrieked beseeching of your will.

After the waving prey is tugged below
to be consumed in secret, beneath the dirt,
the ant lion's slow return looks dreamlike, too.
There's a proprietary fussiness,
meticulous, almost suburban, as
the little killer scrapes his whirlpool smooth.

AN OAK SKINNED BY LIGHTNING

The oak tree skinned by lightning is ringed round
with wood-lice trails on its inmost bark.
The scars of the oak startle: each mark
of its once-hid flesh revels in profound

asymmetry our eyes must dote upon.
The random meanders of the blind wood lice
cut their labyrinthine cicatrice
of cryptic squiggles in soft cambium.

Their carved grooves look like staves and notes of scores
a cello ellipsoidally transmutes
before the main theme flitters to the flutes.
I feel these clear canals. My fingers parse

these worm trails laid bare like epigraphy.
The oak was Christlike as the lightning stripped
its seamless raiment off and the rain whipped
it while it shook, a suffering being, in July

when even dragonfly and hawk moth seem benign.
I am moved by the incommunicable script
of the lightning on the oak tree's swept
pith. Is this the idiolect of summer, the sign

our eyes are aching to decode,
these edicts from a canceled chancery,
these mute communicados of the sensory,
whose each jot seems a letter in a word?

My fingertips Champollion the oak;
the burined lice trails teach my skin.
Here hands alone, not eyes, draw you within
the secretive syllables the lightning struck.

ROOSTER
For Tippy

I like the way the rooster lifts his feet,
so jauntily exact,
then droops one springy yellow claw aloft
just like a tailor gathering up a pleat;
and then there are those small, surprising lilts,
both rollicking and staid,
that grace his bishop's gait,
like a waltzer on a pair of supple stilts
or a Russian on parade.

I like the way he swivels and then slants
his red, demented eye
to tipsy calibrations of his comb
and ogles the barnyard with a shopkeeper's stance.
Sometimes his glossy wattles shudder and bulge
as he bends his feathered ear
and listens, fixed in trance.
When drowsy grubs below the ground indulge
and then stretch up for air,

how promptly he administers his peck,
brisk and executive,
and the careless victim flipflops in his grip!
I like the way his stubby little beak
produces that dark, corroded croak
like a grudging nail tugged out of stubborn wood:
No "cock-a-doodle-doo" but *awk-a-awk*!
He yawps whenever he's in the mood
and the thirst and clutch of life are in his squawk.

Chiefly I love the delicate attention
of the waking light that falls
along his shimmery wings and bubbling plumes
as though light pleasured in tangerine and gentian
or sported like some splashy kid with paints.
But Rooster forms his own cortège, gowns
himself in marigold and shadow, flaunts
his scintillant, prismatic tints—
the poorest glory of each country town.

A CROW AT MORNING

He paces toward our trash pile with a squire's
proprietary stride. Wariness has stropped
his feathers' gloss. He is aubergine
sleekness incarnate. His opulence
stands mittened in a sooty radiance.
O raucous combustion,
uncontained by your own black vanes!
You dignify my morning
with a coal chiaroscuro.
Your flat and avid eye
now gloms some nugget, and you plane
your head with an optician's
click-stop precision, a
strangely childish
flourish
of your Benthamite
beak which brute utility has honed
to its unerring edge. You
lance a bag of ordure, you
dance in, filch and shuddertuft
your head, all
snug yarmulke above your Hasid's
melodious eye.
                    Even so,
your feet (which swag the corners of my eyes)
are pagan feet, nude
to the toes, abutting in bare claws.
Everything is *hefker* to your eyes,
and yet lascivious indigo belies
the Mishnah of your gabardine.

FLAMINGOS

1

My quarrel with your quorum, Monsignor
Flamingo, is that you scant the rubicund
in favor of a fatal petal
tint. I would rather bask
in riots of the roseate
than measure your footfalls'
holy protocols beside the head-
board of a drowsy demiurge.
I think God snores in rose
leaves of serenity, not in your
clatter of cadaverous vermeils.

2

I find flamingos beautiful Tartuffes
who entice as they distance me.
When they display their billiarding
adolescent sprawl of knees I
remember the parochial-
school girls in pink cashmeres, their rosy
kneecaps polished by novenas.

3

Flamingos have the silhouettes
of parking meters. They have no epaulettes
and yet seem always in uniform—
little, stilted caudillos! They swarm
in unruffled ripples of defiling pink.
They mimic ballerinas and yet stink.
Flamingos are dirty in their purity,
blazon Venezuelas of lewd suavity.
Beneath their transcendent, back-bent
legs flamingos are somnolent
and lubricious birds whose stiff tutus
amuse
the spoonbills and anhingas who erect
nests of fish skin to reflect
the imperial smut of the sky.
                         I feel a samba roll
under my eyelids when flamingos stroll
oceanward at sundown and clap their stubs of wings
in gawky, rank, hierophantic posturings.

4

When the Lord God created the flamingos, He
fell into despondency. He knew
that roseate feathers on such skeletons
elicit incredulity. He gloomed
for days, obsessive as a poet who
discovers a covert love affair between
obstreperous syllables and then,
cracking grandeur from the egg of shame,
sets these
diametric desperadoes in a pas de deux.

5

Only in Miami is supreme
loneliness apparent in flamingo dawn.
The squalor of the place is cruelly pink.
There are pink curtains on the lousy shacks.
The impulse to adorn deepens the nakedness.
There, flamingos all the color of a bone
scavenge in vermilion stateliness.
Their pink flocks forage in that loneliness.

ANHINGA

There is a calisthenic finesse to the neck
as the poke-stick of the beak
comes up. The neck's loop revolves,
too sinuous to be plausible.
This neck has innuendoes of a fish,
must writhe and must wriggle and
must pivot in sopping
twists, distinctively drip-dry,
till the rough feathers regain their brackish glare.
Eel spasms, annular
cascades, clamber the bayberry
over the frilled sludge where the gar
gelatinizes in its own repose.
The anhingas ogle the gorgeous sky
over Shark River and as they gaze
extend vespertilian
wings, meticulous and moist.
They hold their pose.
It's almost reverential for those,
like me, with worshipful proclivities
when these black birds spread out such wings.

O anhingas on the floodgates and the levee bridge,
you pray with nothing but water and I see
your signatory darkness cloak the sun.

TURTLE'S SKULL

The shore rang under my naked heel
after the squall: delicate eyelids
of shell, the scattered audacities
limestone confects: those peach-stung
volutes of supersession, cowrie
and turkey wing, the murex with its
acrid spirals and the bony rose
of the lion's paw. Vacancies, all
vivid! Where conch gongs trumpeted
afternoons of disenchantment,
poincianna-hosannas of departure,

I set the bare-scoured skull
of the loggerhead seaward
and at daybreak, when the iron
ladle of the eastern sky oozed its
apricot-bold fissures of day,
scathing water poured
from the eyes of the skull.
Black sockets wept the sea.

COASTLINES

Barnacles cinch
sea-battered pilings.
Dog whelks maraud in mud.
How the North Atlantic
wrangles the rocks!
Above, the houses of the fishermen
look matchstick but are fierce.
They hold to the skittish boulders with all their might.
Next door, in the wired-off
graveyard of the cove,
the headstones lean aslant,
scripture pages thumbed down by the wind.
Below them the ocean
seethes and scathes all day,
all night, and the spray
smokes where it slaps the shore.
Tide pools boil with foam.

On coastlines you realize
what world will last.
See how the lean light
glances against granite.
Erosion gorges the coastline out,
nibbles the gaps.
You feel a shiver in
the ocean's memory.

2

What if this coastal road, these roofs
vivid against the ocean, these
steeples and these gas
stations, what if these docks and piers and
marinas, these tough
white houses with their windowboxes,
stood only in the minute's multitude?
What if each minute made its universe?
What if in our hands we held our world
breakable and rainbow-velveted as mere
wobbling bubbles that our children blow?
I feel my skin, I feel my face,
yield to the light as coastlines yield,
accepting the loving
phosphorescence of daylight's
demarcation. I feel
the violence of all its delicacy.

3

Coastlines are where our opposites ignite
and no one can say, *After all, it's all right.*
Coastlines are where your father and your mother
turn without a word forever from each other.
Coastlines are where the quick-footed sun
touches Ultima Thule and can no longer run.
Coastlines are where we learn the ocean's tragedy:
incessant endeavor, incessant panoply,
broken down to crumbs of nothingness
and yet we want to bless
each ragged repetition of the waves,

so inconsolable, so close to us.

II

The horsemen and the night and the desert know me,
And the sword and the lance, the paper and the pen.
                                    —Abu al-Tayyib al-Mutanabbi

MUTANABBI IN EXILE

Abu al-Tayyib al-Mutanabbi, the greatest of classical Arabic poets, moved from court to court in Syria, Egypt, and Iraq, earning his living as a panegyrist. He was murdered by robbers in 965.

In alien courts I melodied for bread
but now the sordid business of verse
enjoins me to this dry, northern
kingdom where disaffected ostriches
snort at sundown and the prince
idles the hours away with paradigms
in ancient grammar books.

A shabby gentility obscured my youth.
Poverty was a stench I couldn't scrub
and largesse smarted out of others' hands.
But language was immeasurable as shame
and burned in the beatific mouth of God—
He is exalted!—and now language flows
from my fingertips and from my quill
the way the spider tesselates its silk.

My heart is fringed with arrows like the sun
or the chastened, wincing surface of a blade
hammered in Damascus out of Indian steel.
My heart is like the chilly ramparts of cranes
longing southward as the winter dawns.
But my lines still rustle lovely as the slide
of rosaries of olive wood blessed by pilgrimage
or the pages, startled as acacia,
in the whispering codices of the Law.

The moon enacts its faded casuistries
and there are thorn trees twisted like beggars
by the last stones of encampments, the dry
dung of pack animals, and *thumam* grass
stuffed in the fire crevices. There I stopped,
and all my pain swept over me
in that smooth-blown place.
How could such meager anonymous shreds
summon remembrance in a spill of tears?

South of Aleppo, where the stony mesas gust
with desolation and the jackal bitch whimpers
and snuffles in an unloved earth, my longing
rang as hungry as the crows of winter.
The inkwell knows me, and the carven quill,
and the tense and crackling surfaces of parchment,
and swords and lances know me, and the strong horses,
and the night will remember me, and all empty places.

MUTANABBI PRAISES THE PRINCE

The luscious reddening gold of the emir's coin
buys my encomia. I haggle in magnificence,
or then I elbow-dust his aureole.
But such praise costs. The syllables are pearl
nipped from the darkness of Bahrani seas
by clever divers, or rubies of Kashmir
pried from reluctant mines.

Let others gown the prince in obsequious fabrics
or snuggle bracelets and rings of hammered gold
over his wrists and fingers, or incense his hair
with myrrh or labdanum, or dunk his feet
in subtle unguents brought from Hadhramaut.
I garment him in the golden fragrance of praise
that gives men life forever, that will ring
in the shadowy mouths of the unborn,
his great-grandchildren's unimagined progeny,
in chains of consequence effected by the will
of the Compassionate across ungenerated time.

MUTANABBI REMEMBERS HIS FATHER

Sometimes, half in sleep, when the dreaming mind
confuses past and present smokily,
so that dead friends and benefactors turn
and break into smile or greet you, unaware
that everything has changed forever now,
or the unmistakable pressure of a hand
consoles the shoulder of the child you were,
sometimes, then, at such half-realized
encounters, I can picture him again.
The past is knotted like the hempen length
that slides into the midnight of the well.
Each instant survives in darkness lost to us,
perhaps cherished in the mind of the Merciful
the way remembering fingers cherish heirloom pearls.

I picture a man who lurches, like a crab,
up stony alleys, who shudders like a pack mule
under punishing burdens, who sets one wary shoe
before the other as he stumbles and labors along.
Two tipping leather pails bounce on a pole
slung across his arching shoulder blades—
a water carrier, a menial, bent and thonged
to his limber crossbeam, arching like a bow
and he the dark and devastating shaft
ready to fly; or his cramped neck and arms
seem lifted like the hawk's before he stoops.

This man is lashed
to the shame that glitters in his leather buckets
and he squawls all day in his hawker's croak,
"Waw-ter! Pure waw-ter!" A dented cup
bangs at his breastbone. He is himself all
thirst, the parched epitome of the sandy stretch
between Kufa and Samawa, where I parsed my tongue
on redolent paradigms and measured the prosody
of the subtle breezes that fluttered the tent flaps:
mutafa'ilun, mutafa'ilun, fa'ilatun!—
the way grammarians vivisect a verse—
or I lazed to the plangent amber of the oud.

That menial, that lugger of scummy drinks,
his eyes the sooty pink of a slaughter camel's lids,
his mouth cracked and cleft like a winter wadi,
his hands the paws of a Byzantine dancing bear—
that lowest of the low was my papa,
water hauler for the swells of Kinda,
who peddled the stuff of life so I could live
like a prince of Hira in my gem-sewn silks
among the purity of desert tribes whose speech
glittered with the ancient rose-quartz clarity of Adam's tongue.

THE CALIPH

The wily and flamboyant Fatimid, the
intricate Caligula of God, the
neurasthenic delegate of prophets (may
God pray for them!), forbade all women
to wear shoes. He barred the cobblers from
tapping their lasts or battering their little anvils;
only poor prosodists could mime their hammer taps.
This, before he vaporized in the mauve
and umber desert of the air: al-Hakim,
defender of the devious
ambiguity of the Godhead, His penchant for
bagatelles, creator of the paradox
of sharks and swans, Draconian Comedian!

He placed an interdict on
lamentation. He forbade all women to
weep at funerals, rescinded ululations,
and so each black cortège
wound through the lanes of Cairo voicelessly.
Even sorrow is too great a liberty
since it inhabits memory, citadel
beyond the fists of despots, or of God.

And sometimes, in the pitch light of the bazaar,
God's shadow baited bears or egged men on
to braggadocio or fisticuffs, or spied upon
their most secretive gestures, their least
askance innuendoes, their cupped whisperings;
till, surrogate, he evanesced on the Muqattam Hills
one evening, leaving only slivered veils behind.

Perhaps only the forbidden know
the unshod deprivations of the dead,
and perhaps only children who've just learned to walk
savor the nakedness of heels and soles.
Perhaps only the mad
value the little freedom of the shoes.

III

As a tiny seed you sleep in what is small
And in the vast you vastly yield yourself.
                    —Rilke, *The Book of Hours*
                         tr. Stephen Mitchell

ORIGINS

I wanted to go down to where the roots begin,
to find words nested in their almond skin,
the seed-curls of their birth, their sprigs of origin.

At night the dead set words upon my tongue,
drew back their coverings, laid bare the long
sheaths of their roots where the earth still clung.

I wanted to draw their words from the mouths of the dead,
I wanted to strip the coins from their heavy eyes,
I wanted the rosy breath to gladden their skins.

All night the dead remembered their origins,
All night they nested in the curve of my eyes,
And I tasted the savor of their seed-bed.

GRAVEDIGGERS' APRIL

In winter we comfort our dead with talk.
We entertain them with our idle gossip.
We whisper the news while our breath freezes.
We line up at the storage shed where their bodies lie
awaiting the great thaws of uncertain spring.
We tell them how the frost was dark this year
and steep, how business perked up at the quarries,
what happened to those botanists after the avalanche. . . .

The padlock on their door is lumpy
with a blackened ice
but our damp spurts of breath revive
the grieving hinges. Murmurous petals of frost
cloud the numbed metal.
                              And quicker now,
more hurried, as the whisperers file
behind the convenience store:
                              How a yellow stray
littered beneath the baptistry and defiled the stones
and was drowned with all her brood, how Coleman saw
crows build nests of unknown wood in the old foundry,
how hailstones fell for three days laced with blood. . . .

It's comforting to chat even if
no answers return. The winter shapes our words.
The widower drinks, the widow squeezes shut
her eyes, imagining the bluish stain
corruption spreads across a loved complexion.
Come back! they whisper, *I'm lonesome here without you!*
But then, as the winter drags, *I'm glad you're there*
at last . . . where I can love you finally. . . .

Beyond the door they lie
snug in their salt till spring. Some prefer
the new crematory in Schenectady, but for most
of us winter is unthinkable without
the long peace of our conversations.

In April, when the gravediggers return,
staggering, soused to the gills, on overtime,
and the black lock thaws into rusty rain
and they bear them out through the open shed
into the flowering cemetery,

then we can mourn.

HAND-PAINTED CHINA

The slender cake plates had such fiery rims.
They caught the lazy radiance
of afternoons, like torch-
light from a tomb. The old
roses opened to my eyes
their bold, embellished centers
where a soft darkness had
been stippled in. They drew down
my gaze until I felt
labyrinthed in sweetness, like a bee.

My great-aunts painted these.
The hesitant brush strokes on their
undersides read "1893."
The greenness of their china does not fade
but witnesses an opulence the more forlorn
for being without issue. The pinks
and gilts, the raveled petals
blowsy with magenta, importune
the fingers to partake of them.

These were the gravy boats of plenteous
expectation, the creamers rich with dream;
these were the banquet platters, these the
hard yet fragile saucers, of trousseaux.
These were the delicate dishes no one used.
Now they snag the curious
light of afternoons
in magisterial shadow
like a pharaoh's mouth.
                              Here,
in the lovingly abrasive, gently gritted
impasto of hand-painted surfaces
that resist, like skin, with almost plush aplomb,
I feel some embodiment of all
their expectations had the right to claim;
I feel their tentative fingertips touch mine.

SPIDER SILK

Once, when I gashed my finger, Grandmother
led me to the closet down the hall.
There towels and bedsheets lay in fragrant folds
and an old, outgrown doll with bright-blink eyes
that scared me stiff with its hilarity
bled sawdust from its mouth onto a shelf.
Grandma pulled me close to her until
I understood the comfort of her touch.
She poked her free hand in the crevices
and spooled a spiderweb around her nails.
She wound the web again around my wound.
She daubed it tenderly until the clots of silk
touched my blood, and then my bleeding stopped
almost at once.
              There, among the smell of sheets,
in the cold, fresh, dark place that had scared me so,
Grandmother gave me her most secret smile.
Since that day,
learning to love the doubleness of things,
I think the spider silk is in my blood.

THE SUITORS OF
MY GRANDMOTHER'S YOUTH

At dusk on sabbath afternoons the slow-
voiced suitors came, with awkward hat brims in
their field-burred hands. They tipped themselves
on the very brinks of the Sunday chairs.
Their napes were fiery under their collar starch.
The knees of their blue serge suits looked rubbed and smooth.

Fireflies would be blinking then, across the lawns.
Under the hedge, like small and sleepy stars
witnessed through mist, they glittered and went out.
And everywhere, lilac would spire in June
its chaste and promissory fragrance. Her
sisters broke off sprays and clasped them
with half-ironic passion to their throats.
The boys were mute, traded long-suffering,
conspiratorial looks. On slow, speechless
strolls their beaux would hand to them
desperate fistfuls of wild violets,
and all their futures still appeared
benign with promise, all their loves
still hovered before the transactions of the blood.

THE GOSSIP OF THE FIRE

When Grandfather told us stories we
bunched up close, until our shoulders touched
before the fireplace and as near the fire
as respect for its irascible
outbursts would allow. Grandfather's words
kept time with the fire that snapped
in the grate. Firecrackers of sap
punctuated his thoughtful pauses.
The rhythm of the fire was intimate
and drew the whole world in. Outdoors,
beyond the gossip of the fire, he said,
the creatures of the field stood listening,
drawing some pensive pleasure from
the crafty coincidence of voice and blaze.
As Grandfather told his story we
pictured the animals, beyond the bright,
breathing beside us as our shoulders touched.

He spoke and a bullfrog's amber
eyeballs held the moon. A red fox
with his curt, alacritous ears
alert
was savoring some specially resinous phrase.
The hens in their cozy ammoniac coop
felt eggs emerging as his words emerged.

The creatures of the field, like us,
were witnesses,
attentive and yet vulnerable as those
who witnessed without voice at Calvary,

and their eyes were radiant with anecdote.

FINDING A PORTRAIT OF
THE RUGBY COLONISTS,
MY ANCESTORS AMONG THEM

It is as if you held them all, as God
must have held them when He made their
mouths, their shoulders, their irreplaceable
eyes. It is as if their world were in your hands,
here, in this rectangular beechwood frame
with the brown paper backing that complains like flame
with crackling annoyance when you tug the wire,
bright-twisted, that sustained it on some wall.
There is a Godlike feeling to encompass so
on a flat, embrittled print their many lives,
though only in effacement can you hope
to sustain their least regard.
                              To enter this
beech-embrasured instant when a lens
with curatorial dispassion caught
their momentary countenances asks
the modesty of trustful ignorance.
And though you cannot know them, yet you feel
bone-closeness to their lives.
                              Tell me, if you had been
the God who shaped their cheekbones
and their brows, the dignified alertness
of their ears, their ceremonial and
formal smiles, their throats the patience of a
May sun mottled with its little dabs of luminance,
the fingers curved on Bibles or on canes,
the feet in their black-thonged propriety
of dainty boots or strenuous clodhoppers,
would you, for a world,
have let them tumble into
nothingness and seen their strong hearts rot,
or would you have raised them up again,
the way you rouse a sleeper or a child?

FOR A MODEST GOD

That fresh towels invigorate our cheeks,
that spoons tingle in allotted spots,
that forks melodion the guested air,
that knives prove benign to fingertips,
that our kitchen have the sweet rasp of harmonicas,
that stately sloshings cadence the dishwasher,
that lobsters be reprieved in all the tanks
and mushrooms fetched from caverns for the light,
and that the oil of gladness glisten down
the chins of matriarchs, anoint the crib;
that there be aprons of capacious cloth
enveloping the laps of nimble chefs,
that our sauces thicken on the day of fasts,
that the hearth cat frisk his whiskers and attend,
that no domestic terror smite our minds,
that midnights be benignant with a god's
oven mitts and spatulas and solace-broths:
a little god, a little modest god, a
godkin in a shriven cupboard, Lares-
palmable and orderly, presiding
over the hierarchies of the silverware,
our platters' strata and our serving spoons;
a small dull god, ignorant of thunder,
attuned to nothing somberer than the trills
when all our crockery trembles to the fault
of obscure, dimly rumorous calamities.

RAIN IN CHILDHOOD

On schooldays, when the windows of the bus
dimmed with all our breath, we pressed up close
in jostling slickers, knowing the pleasure of
being a body with other bodies, we children
a flotilla of little ducks, paddling together
on the wet ride to the schoolhouse door.
Once there, now toweled and dry, we looked outside
back where the hot, vociferous rain still fell
and stooped the trees and swung the traffic light
and pocked the yellow crosswalks till they fizzed
with all their gritty torrents to the curb.

That steamy tar-damp smell of morning rain,
its secret smokiness upon our mouths,
surprised us with some sorrow of nostalgia.
Our past already had such distances!
Already in that fragrance we could taste
the end of childhood, where remembrance stands.

And when thunder pummeled the embrittled clouds—
concussive ricochets that made the teacher
hover with the chalk held in her hand—
we saw the lightning lace the school's facade
with instantaneous traceries and hairline fires,
like a road map glimpsed by flashlight in a car.

IV

Blut ist ein ganz besondrer Saft.
(Blood's a very peculiar juice.)
—Goethe, *Faust* I, line 1740

BAUDELAIRE TO MME. AUPICK,
AT HONFLEUR (1867)

Chère Madame, do you remember still
the windows to the garden where we sat
watching the sun on August afternoons
lovingly ascend the leafy wall
as though it touched with radiance
each object in its path: the tall
stems of dahlias, the trellises
where coiled brambles of young roses hung,
the statue of a nymph with hollow shell
splashing the glittered water toward a pool
where indolent carp swam in shadowy calm
until the sun's long declination shone
along the ripples that their bright fins caused?
Our conversations had the harmony
of that ascending light. A tacit
concord spoke from simple things.

When I remember those long afternoons,
the way the sunlight gently touched your hair,
its infinitely tender kiss
upon your lips and cheeks and eyelashes,
it seems to me our conversations were
accompanied by light, were luminous,
and every word we spoke
assumed serene embodiment in all
the voiceless objects that around us stood—
the linen with its darkly sparkling
folds, the heavy luster of the silverware,
the dense roses in their crystal mirroring
the calm crimson of the setting sun.

If I imagine Eden or a paradise
where passion steeps its secret harmonies,
my memory is of those soft afternoons
when without speaking, or the need to speak,
the two of us admired the fading light.
Those were the last times that we had of such
order made passionate in lucidity,
of passionate innocence, passionate peace,
a love not governed by the torturers.

SALLE DES MARTYRS

You see where blessed Théophane was nailed
to a ceremonial plank in mockery
of the crucifix he brought benighted souls
and how expertly the Mandarin's men sawed
his anointed limbs, one by one, away. It is
the love, in these depictions of
his mutilations, which most horrifies.
Wherever mere agony fails to persuade,
some clumsy well-meant brush stroke puddles
the dipped blood. His silken slippers
discolor in the reliquary
darkness of the Martyrs' Room among
pyx, monstrance, and ciborium, the
golden home of the shriek.
He wrote: "Only the weak
are winnowed out for martyrdom."

We stare at his stark remains under glass—
his thongs and worm-riddled breviary,
his rosary with all its silvery
decades yet intact. And here, in a nearby
case beneath the gravelly loudspeaker, we
may find the instruments we used to use
on one another: the rust-serrated words,
the garotte of indifference, the swords
of our separate nights, the grudging thumb-
screws of speechlessness, and that so slow
obliviating boot that grinds out love.

No tableaux will commemorate our loss,
no delicate daubs of calligraphy our crown.
The prerecorded messages wind down.
Beyond the blood-freckled alb and chasuble
an eighteenth-century Christ, all ivory,
fissures upon His cross.
And outside, in the moist Parisian noon,
the rosebushes draw their redness from this room.

BLOOD
For Danny and Chuck

1

All night in your ears you'll hear the blood sing
I am king!   *I am king!*   *I am king!*

You'll hear the ganged hammers of the blood erect
its palaces. You'll feel the sluices of the blood connect

its empires. Blood with its royal, rotten scent,
in its rush-lit vestments, in its vehement

arabesques, dangles its scarlet manacles
or glows like radium inside sly ventricles.

In stables where no savior lays his head
blood shows its Balkan, its Rwandan, red.

Blood is apodictic in its contradictions,
cascades from Adam's heart the crimson fictions

of tribes and clans and families,
knots the sinews with hot pieties.

2

Children not of my blood but of my love,
whose sweet sonship is compounded of

all that mutual breath could make of hours,
we have plaited together what is ours

minute by minute. Consanguinity
knows nothing of our fierce fragility.

Blood relies
hysterically on old school ties

while our enlacements all have been made
thread by thread, braid upon braid.

3

When lawyers with their starry
writs and decrees of certiorari

banter your nativity,
haggling some clotted pedigree,

Say, Blood should be slow, should be slow,
sound chuckle-melodic in heart's bungalow,

be the hearthstone made rich by sweet hemagogues,
the murmurous marrow of soft synagogues.

Let the vessels' cantillations in your throat
dulcimer the temples' pulsing note.

For necklaces of ancestors twine love knots of time.
Backward to Eden let our recognitions rhyme.

CRAB

Before dying the old woman became crab-
like. Her spotted hand backs became
algae-emeralded. "How pretty I
am!" she said. But her big
toe, with its violet spur
of crimped nail, clicked
in pincer snips, and she
screamed. Only her soft
mouth that had loved to suck
oysters and grapes amazed
her with its red machinery
of appetite. I saw her slow
serene eyes shinny up their
stems.
      A crab, and sunset-
crimson as a crab, her hunched
belly glittered. Only in her
bath was there still
that drowned flower of helplessness.
I watched her scuttle breathing
sideways to say, "How pretty
I am!" I hated
her crabbedness, even while I comforted
the alert pinnacles where her grieving
eyes began. But "Nobody
can forgive
you now," she
hissed.

HATE

Hate is so bracing and accommodates
insight cozily. Hate icicles
the eyes. A happy hate rejuvenates,
gladdens hair, brightens cheeks, bicycles
nimbly with the gusto of unchagrined exuberance.
An heirloom hatred's fun as well, accretes
in limestone ziggurats of bane. Hate lets you dance
on your own bones at last, and hate secretes

warm poisons, lovely but so lonely
venoms that pretext a hidden wish.
Obverse snugness of hate is only
like love in that it's not squeamish
at all; grasps in a rush, with sleek grace:
to mangle, or to caress, the other's face.

AMBER
For Irena

Prismed by amber, the insect's wing
curves outward in a resinous nonchalance.
Casual fatality has paused in its dance.
I am tenderest when I touch this glozened thing.

Time's imagination stumbles me,
the way time tastes the roof beam's future ruin
or calibrates the hovering, faint tune
in the siskin's wingbeat, with its brief veracity.

The stillness of surviving objects pleases
our reveries. The inarticulate
obduracy of a tigrine chip of agate
spilled from a misplaced cuff link seizes

our attention, so mere things appear
stationary, resistant, and impervious.
The opera glasses, pearl-lensed, that will outlive us
accord a terrible pleasure of mortality. We're

cruelly honored in our transience,
evanescent instances of some unique
reticulation. I hear you speak
close to my ear. I feel your diffidence

as you slip your clothes and then your jewelry
and press against me till our nakedness
warms us with momentous gentleness
and we lie hidden in that clarity.

HISTORY

This is our history.
The place is empty now where we began.
The rooms are full of sunlight, and the sea
effaces all the traces where we ran.

I dreamt about the world before I was,
that darkened curve of shore, the stark
clarity of coral undersea. Does
broken coastline demarcate the dark

of unbeginning daylight? Now I see
the twining light with all the dark I can.
This is our history:
The place is empty now where we began.

PART TWO
FROM *BAVARIAN SHRINE AND OTHER POEMS* (1990)

Only curving praise of rain
Lifts the still gesture into green.
    —Paul R. Hoffmann,
        "The Snail of Trees"

STARFISH

The stellar sea-crawler, maw
concealed beneath, with offerings of
prismed crimson now darkened, now like
the smile of slag, a thing made rosy
as poured ingots, or suddenly dimmed—

I appreciate the studious labor
of your rednesses, the scholarly fragrance
of your sex. To mirror tidal drifts
the light ripples across or to enhance darkness
with palpable tinctures, dense as salt.

You crumple like a puppet's fist
or erect, bristling, your tender luring barbs.
Casual abandon, like a dropped fawn glove.
Tensile symmetries, like a hawk's claw.

You clutch the sea floor.

You taste what has fallen.

RAILYARD IN WINTER

The colors of disused railyards in winter;
the unnamed shades of iron at four o'clock;
the sun's curiosity along abraded stones;
corrosion that mimes the speckled lichen of woods;
the islands of stubbly rust on padlocked doors;
the fierce shoots of winter grass among cinders;
the fragile dim light, infused with tannin,
that falls clear on the stamped bottle glass
and regales the cast-off boot.
                   The colors of shale
cratered with dark rain. The rough knots
of crabgrass near the steps to the loading dock
and their sandy, scruffed umber.
                        The hues
of all negligible things: the nugatory blue
of slag chunks between the ties. Then, the smell
of those resinous blisters of red on the fence,
like a childhood of pines.
                   Such unpeopled places
luxuriate on Sundays. What was made for use
discloses in uselessness its transient magic,
assumes the radiance of the useless grasses.

SKUNK CABBAGE

The skunk cabbage with its smug and opulent smell
opens in plump magnificence near the edge
of garbage-strewn canals, or you see its shape
arise near the wet roots of the marsh.
How vigilant it looks with its glossy leaves
parted to disclose its bruised insides,
that troubled purple of its blossom!
It always seemed so squat, dumpy and rank,
a noxious efflorescence of the swamp,
until I got down low and looked at it.
Now I search out its blunt totemic shape
and bow when I see its outer stalks
drawn aside, like the frilly curtains of the ark,
for the foul magenta of its gorgeous heart.

SPIDER

I caught a spider sucking a drink
from the kitchen sponge. Its thirst
disgusted me. I didn't want to know
how our requirements coincide.
Still, it was almost beautiful
as the spider stepped from the wet sponge
and swung into the pot of mint,
where I knew
it would rest and hide and savor
the cool taste of water
in its dark mouth.

LAZARUS IN SKINS

After his long recovery, Lazarus
began wearing lizard-skin boots.
He sported cravats of rich kid
and black lustrous jackets of young calf.
He couldn't endure the cling
of fabric, the insinuations of silk.
Even textiles woven of moth-soft cloth
aggravated his dreams.
Not suffering, he said, but hope
had made him hysterical and vain.
Now he desired the sinuous
space of other skins, those fresh
folds of amplitude, the beautiful
blueness of snakes' eyes, cloud
lenses, when they shed their last skin.

FORGETFUL LAZARUS

Lazarus forgot his gloves, and the blots
on his numb fingers showed too white.
He forgot the injustices of his shoes;
the lichens on his toes began to glow.
Lazarus could not remember to cover his mouth;
the gray smell of his entombment coiled out.
He also forgot his sky-blue tinted lenses
that made his sunken eyeballs shine with life.
He forgot to scrape away his death
that laced his arms and legs, his cheeks—
vivid and difficult as the rose-rich gills of fish—
with delicate ruffles of fungus, with sweet mold.

LAZARUS LISTENS

The relentless waltzes of the Golden Age
Retirement Club upstairs left him no peace.
All night their scything strings rippled his nerves
attuned to spider sighs and beetle whisperings.
All night he heard parades
and festivals, fiestas where rude shoes
finessed their sad mazurkas into dawn.
And then at dawn he heard the pure
arpeggios of hooligans in stairwells
or his ears, pitched
to the yawns of moths,
followed the thin, self-conscious lullabies
of senile women in their flowered chairs,
cradling the surprise of light.

He was inert as earth,
simple as sand, consummate as clay,
the driest obstacle, the echo nest
against which all their music dumbly beat.

LAZARUS AND BASEMENTS

Lazarus had been a sluggish kid
fond of musky crevices where moles
doze or where opossums paw their sour
disreputable nests. He loved
that asylum of old clothes where moths
web the spotted lightbulb or the crawl
cellar where the fat exterminator went
on his monthly trips.
                                    At night he saw
spiders in his sleep, and dream itself
furled outward in tough silk from the sly
spinnerets of sleep. When he died,
they planted him in a damp and mildewed hole.
His basement nature had come home at last.

Imagine our surprise
not at his wet, still-bandaged face
by the grave's low door,
nor the rank and vicious stink
that smoked from his shroud,
but at his loving familiarity with the damp,
and the companionable clasp of his arms,
brimming with vermin,
and all the gray caresses of his twittering friends.

LAZARUS IN SUMATRA

*But what thinks Lazarus? Can he warm his blue hands by holding them
up to the grand northern lights? Would not Lazarus rather be in Sumatra
than here?*

—Melville, *Moby-Dick*

I wanted to warm his blue hands;
I tried to rub the life back
into his flat cheeks, his slack jaw.
See, I whispered, the sun
abrades the rippled roof
and strops his coroner's claws
against the rain. . . .
Did I want to shock him back
to life, with all its imprecations?

The ground is damp and sandy;
graves are scooped out of dunes.
The strict sun does not revive
but desiccates all that it falls across:
I felt him toughen, turn stringy.

He was a thing out of place
in that simulacrum of paradise,
like the skull of a doll.

He was so wind-shorn, so weather-bent,
he had become such drift,
such plangent bone,
his complexion the stark of chalk.

Death, here,
means curling back into that
simplicity of shape—
S-curve, nascent parabola,
the little ellipses of the bones—
corrective to the sun's extravagance:

a loyalty to one's own first dimensions.

LICHENS

Between the stones, by the sea's edge,
and in sheltered hollows of the rock,
flat lichens cling. Their surfaces are gray,
dry and crinkly. Some are cracked and sharp
or flake away like weathered paint in strips.
They survive the cold light and the spray
torn from the North Atlantic. The way they clasp
and cover the rocks seems to signify
inconspicuous courage and tenacity. But
at evening they gleam bleakly in exact
configurations, and their order is fiercer
than the sea's: their drab arabesques
look splotchy, rust-wept or scaly as dead bark;
far off, they're starlike, spiky as galaxies.
Like us they clutch and grip their chilly homes
and the wind defines their possibilities.

CRANEWORLD

When the sandhill crane resolves
to hatch her universe, emphatic
designs impose on her angle of view.
Her innate notions are splashy but few.
The blueprint of craneworld involves
thatchiness, a prickledom of aromatic
nestnesses. It is spatulate and concave
together, and is conspicuous in fish.

In craneworld the sun is both god and slave
and the night rises in the darkness of the eye
itself.
        Frogs' voices console her cosmos lavish-
ly, and there is the strong calendar of sky
southward.
        Her inwardness is spherical, grit-white,
concentric in its cadences, with gravities of light.

RIVER PLANTS

1: WHITE WATERLILIES

The waterlilies have a jagged look,
spiky as aloes or the blades of palms,
and yet seem almost bridal in their whitenesses.
Within, a diffidence of faint
saffron shows, like the first intimations
of morning or that almost indiscernible
gold of willows at the start of spring.

The waterlilies ride the detours and
dead ends of the river where the current
stalls and pools. Their petals open rigidly
like the lacquered eyelashes of dolls.
Beside them, their wide flat leaves
wobble with disparate water drops that roll
like puzzled mercury on terrazzo floors.
They seem so still, ethereal and virginal.
Their fragrance is cold and white as their blooms.
Only when you lean to look within
will you see the avid bees
stagger in their yellow pollen.

2: BULLHEAD LILY

Like the sagging dial of a broken clock
the bullhead lily dangles its gold
globular blossom above the stream.
The single flower bobs and wands on its
resilient stem, right-angled to the crimped
calm of its lily pad, which seems to disavow
its bold and nodding yellow, its bulbous
and insistent talon of petals.
The lily looks like a crab's eye on its stalk
or a periscope probing upward from the mud
or like a scepter in a dozing hand.
But all such similes slide and fall away
into the water where the lily grows
while its river-jostled shadow slants across
the cold circumference of its drifting leaves.

Once on a sandbar near a bend in the creek
I found a bullhead lily washed up in pale muck
and saw how its lank tubes of roots, spongy
and venous in the unaccustomed sun,
assembled the mud, fisted its sufficiency
of sand, as though its grip sustained
the shifting river darkness where it clung.

3: PICKERELWEED

The sketchy stands of pickerelweed
that oversee the river's surface have
a lazy grace of curious alertness.
They seem to gaze away from shore,
especially in midsummer when their small
successive petals begin to form.
The newer blossoms continuously surmount
the dead and fading petals on the stem.
They sentinel the riverbank with scuffed
steeples of attentive lavender
that show a bruised fluorescence as the day
climbs. At noon, the flowers pale,
become inconspicuous, until the evening stream
discloses a shading almost porphyry
in their ragged pinnacles.
                                    At summer's end
the rhizome where their cool, slim stalks ascend
coils in upon itself. The leaves are marked
with calligraphic patterns of decay
like the labyrinthine signatures
on ancient bronzes tarnished by the air.
There is a sense of stealth and
supersession in the leaves.
After the frost has singed and stiffened them,
the leaves retract and curl, then crumple down
like heirloom scarves that moths have spoiled.

WOOD FUNGUS

juts in gray hemispheres like a horse's lip
from tree trunks. The outer edge is crimped
in sandy ripples and resembles surf.
The upper plane of the fungus does not shine
but is studious beige and dun, the hue
of shoe soles or the undersides of pipes.
Jawbone-shaped, inert as moons, neutral
entablatures, they apron bark and pool
rain. Underneath, they're darker, fibrous
and shagged.
                    Mountain artists like to etch
delicate patterns on their flat matte skins,
and their tobacco-bright sketch marks look burnt
as tattoos or tribal tangles of scars.
When you grip their surfaces, they bruise.
When you pry them from their chosen oak,
they seem shut fast, like the eyes of sleepers,
or the tensed eyelids of children when they're scared.

FOUNDRY

Beyond the abandoned foundry
the ground of the dried-up creek
is littered with blue chunks of slag.
Sometimes you spot a snake,
dry as those glassy fragments,
sliding among the refuse heaps
but shiny as unexpected water,
where everything in July is parched and white.
I cherish the curls and brusque escarpments
of what was lopped and pared
from cooling pig iron on the hissing floor
a hundred years back—
those gritty amethysts of slag.

In the shade of the casting house
I worked a hand-wrought nail
out of a powdery corner.
Delicate flakes of corrosion
brightened my fingertips.
The air had the taste of old
iron reddened by the dryness of time.
In its harsh twist
the nail gave back
the heat and labor of its forging
like fierce light from long-dead stars.

MOTHS AT NIGHTFALL

The moths alarmed us.
They were big and dark and they clung
against the screen at night
like starving children.
They were intent on the light
inside and afterward, the banal
lamps seemed marvelous in our eyes:
for hours, Grandma's cherished silk table lamp
with its soiled pink shade
glowed against their darkness
like a signal fire.
                    The moths'
ancient eyes had a slick black glitter
in the inaccessible brightness of parlors.
Their huge madras wings, graced
with a dusty haze of pollen,
pulsed so slowly upon the screen
all night. And their stark
delicacy of fringed and pluming
antennae, keen to the most
distant perfumes, enthralled
and repelled: they curved like white
ferns banished from the daylight,
or sometimes, as we watched them,
their feathery antennae furled outward
and seemed to tremble with attention,
vivid against the darkened yard beyond.

STATUES AND MANNEQUINS

1

The populous bronzes of our city
doze greenly as winter draws on.
History topples in inconspicuous
atoms of displacement—oh, slowly, by
schedules nestled in the foundry's
neglected archives.
                    But the mannequins
sport perfect cream-tinted breasts
and alluring alcoves of thigh,
and they gesture sandily in a time
inaccessible to us—their eyes, how
their eyes appear to seek shape and
finality, as though their designer
impressed them with the jocular blessing
of his consummate thumb!
                    Incorruptible,
unseasonal, their vivid shades drift
glibly, unscarred by the bright corrosions
statues shoulder in their dying greenery.

2

From the twirled labyrinth of the finger-
print, enigmatic as a ritual bronze
vessel (the massive purity of a Shang ewer
with its hieratic tiger's face), the sheer
ethereal vectors of their lives appear.
The anonymity of night has coronated them.
A namelessness as lustral as the dawn
invests them with sepals of nobility,
vivifying, quick, acclamatory—

But these are brittle with the temporary,
accommodate the sea flash torn from cloud,
gather their adoration in the sundown hour
when snowflakes batten on the iron lamps,
and have the lacquered isinglass of hurt
all negligible surfaces collect.

3
Because I loved their statuesque and votive
stances, mere palettes for the stern couturier,
I graced their monochrome with mental
harpstrings, grotesque in their slender
melodies, and let imagination venerate
the classic shadows of their chins and ears.
The postures of mannequins are gossamer,
while the heavy haunches of the monuments
clutch cement and hunker down for ice.

All that dreaded life in me admired
the serene sterility of mannequins.
All that evaded love in me preferred
their oratorical instant to the dim
encumbrances of November and the slow
disfigurement of moments that wear down
the willed fragility of all our monuments.

4

There is another world beneath the eyes
of statues, where horizons hold
the drowsy verdigris of disenchantment.
There is another life in the open hands
of triumph with its blind stigmata of rust.
The biting rain of late November
corrodes their falcon pupils, lenses
trained on essences.

                       Behind snug glass,
in the pampered habitats of mannequins,
the smarting contortions of the seasons
appear as captivating as cascades.
The ornamental fountains of decay
that blush the momentary fingertips
with coral shadows, sea suffusions,
gentle the imagination.

                       Mannequins betray
the patriarchal eyelids of the snow.

5

The lost gesture of the statue, that
hesitation in glory, what ran from our
fingers in the plazas of remembrance—
sometimes, even here, where the sour
winter circles, there is a fragrance
of the sea conveyed by the grieving
stones from the matrix of their origin,
or an iron wind offers the smell of the sea
from the east.
               Why were the works
of our hands brittle as November,
fugitive as the sparse light that falls
over houses crouched against the cold?
Sometimes when the shrill silver
of a moon sounds its bitter voluntary,
we feel it all along our skin;
our shoulders assume that momentary
majesty of tremulous codices, that
piquant surface of the temporary
skin, inscribed by the vivid light.

FINGERNAILS

It is the patrimony of reptiles, or of birds,
to possess such pale claws, to sport such
little flashes of keratin at the farthest tip
of the grasp. The baby hoatzin has archaic
claws along its barbarous wings
that boost it into the Peruvian trees;
so, too, our reminiscent hooks
that let our fingertips negotiate
the air, and that curve around so
obediently, like shields at rest, with
all the snug patience of a carapace,
snail's armature, or the fastidious
hermit crab's limping pagoda of shell.
The manicurist lovingly rebukes
the creeping cuticle so that the faint
crescents, like clouds along horizons,
reappear. The fingernails are suffused
with the blood's sweet light,
though the nails of the newly dead
possess a terrible hailstone
opacity. The fingernails palisade
the unruly ranks of our willful fingers,
and whenever we clasp our hands
a brief convivial darkness sheathes our nails.

NOSE

The nose is antithetical. It sniffs,
snuffles, wallows in sneezes, then recoils
in Roman nobility, profile-proud;
pampers its fleshy shadow in bas-
reliefs; or is serenely alcoved within
rotunda where the chiseled light
dapples its expansive flanges.
                                        Nose
is tuberous, rootlike, with subsoil
affinities, has its own mossy
aromas, feels bulbous as corms or
crimped as rhizomes but, even so,
stands graced with little wings above
the harbored nostrils.
                                The nose
sunders the face in symmetry,
bisects us in hemispheres where selves
negotiate along the boundary lines
of smiles or scowls.
                                All night,
in the snug bed of the face,
the nose exults.

BAVARIAN SHRINE

1

The rusted feet of Christ in roadside shrines
where the eager nail has bled into the stone
transform the tough-hewn birch that disciplines.

His agony is fossilized in red
lichens of corrosion on pale linden wood.

The old-time craftsmen carved Him like a goose
with slathered ribs that spew out lymph and pus.
Three lurid ulcers colonize His thigh.
Pustules of malachite surround each eye.
A loving laceration smears His mouth.
Affection and the brute regard for truth
suture His temples with the maggot's twists.
The black iron spikes surge from His wrists.

And yet for me this victim, tethered like
a swan, is lewd and holy:

                              O Thou
peacock of decay. . . .

2

The spotted hogs trot past to the abattoir.
Their flanks are mired with fear dung and they squeal.
Their pink noses snuffle the poignant air.
Men club the hogs with black padded hammers,
then swing them up on hooks and stab their throats.
Their shrieks are inconsolable and mad.
Their eerie voices give the shrine its cry.
Pilgrim, you shudder, stung by hurt and fear.
The thighs of Christ are burnished and severe.
A murderous perfection lights His eye.

A downy princess texture to the skin—
only the exquisite can savor pain—
the royal exclamations of a flame
that feeds most fiercely on the tutored nerve.
Aristocratic in His gilded Calvary:
did the numb peasants worship in His form
the hated bodies of their feudal lords,
imagining beneath the ermine cloaks
flesh that could whimper to the flail's white strokes?

3

The pretty little hogs with speckled sides,
their fernlike ears scrolled over clever eyes,
that pick a delicate path on trotting hooves
across the trash and mud of a weathered sty,
enthralled me as I knelt before the shrine.
(I share the German fondness for their swine.)

In autumn, when they come to butcher them, I
memorize their long, despairing squeals
that fill the Bauernhof. I smell their blood,
the stink of singeing bristle, and the smoke,
but feel the most for those who cannot cry,
who wedge their frightened bodies to the fence
and shake with dumbstruck terror, paralyzed
and staring, or expel quick spurts of nervous dung
that stains their patterned haunches and stiff tails.

And afterward, just past the killing ground,
I watched a hunting spider trap the flies
invited by the reek of thickened blood;
her dust-embedded web only an instrument,
all wonder butchered, pure function manifest,
with jags of dark heart's blood snagged on the strands.

[86]

DECEMBER

December rings in the chill mouths of bells,
the shadowy solicitude of grasses
eyelashed with precarious snow.
There is a crystalline insistence in the black
repetitious rooftops with their shock
of snow. The ragged chimneys seem
to pray with fingers pinched
together in entreaty while the luscious
clouds of winter wallow on gray
organzas of sundown.
                      December bows
under threadbare memories. The spider
in the corner of the house shrivels
to a small dark claw. At night
our dreams infringe and pool,
our common terrors shake us in sleep.

Upriver there are remote
oceans whose cold waves still ring
like freezing echoes in the mouths of bells.

CONCH SHELL

1

The conch shell on our kitchen counter leans
sideways on its spiky, flaring lip,
displaying a pinkish, petal-like interior.
The outer shell, much grittier,
still has its papery membrane, a brown caul
flaking away in tatters. This reminds us
that our shell is not mere ornament
but once housed some unappealing, pale
worm or sluglike being;
one of those slippery, spittle-
mantled creatures who construct, laborious
in secretion, such begonia-plush
palaces of glory.

Shells are paradoxical the way they draw
the eye, and then the fingertips, inside.
When we peek inside the conch shell,
there is a sloping balustrade of faint
pink before the darkness, almost like a bare
shoulder glimpsed briefly in a window frame.
When we look within, the final light
dissolves in shadow, just as once we peered
upward to where the staircase of our childhood
spiraled into the dark.

The conch is the trumpet of solemn festivals
and its pinnacle—auger-threaded,
spire-sleek, piquant as lance
tip, or the brass casque of a khan—
scalpels the roughened currents asunder.
But the russet life that hides inside,
whose flesh tastes good in broths,
flinches from the light.

The secret fabricator of itself,
refusing to be known
by anything beyond the dawn-pink
shell that houses and articulates
its lithe inhabitant—
how that small, crawling diffidence,
the slime-wreathed animal that flows,
a pygmy to its own magnificence,
inches ocean runnels, seraphically akimbo!
This recluse with a flare for ostentation,
glabrous and glistening, secure in glory
that it secretes but cannot see,
emblems a self in its configuration.

I've seen conchs docked and husked,
stripped of their calcareous splendor, plump
amorphous things, arching, like tongues
torn from mouths or some hidden
shapelessness of desire drawn into the sun.
I've seen the unrecognizable architect
of itself marketed in dripping baskets,
leaving behind nothing but the pale
pulsing of remembered oceans
in the veiled shell's proclamatory lip.

MY MOTHER IN OLD AGE

As my mother ages and becomes
ever more fragile and precarious,
her hands dwindle under her rings
and the freckled skin at her throat
gathers in tender pleats like some startled fabric.
The blue translucence of her veins gives
the texture of her skin an agate gleam,
and the dark blue, almost indigo
capillaries of her cheeks and forehead
resemble the gentle roots
of cuttings of violets
in sheltered jars.
                        I love her now more urgently
because there is an unfamiliar and relentless
splendor in her face that terrifies me.

"Oh, don't prettify decrepitude,"
she demands. "Don't lie!
Don't make old age seem so *ornamental*!"

And yet she abets her metamorphosis,
invests herself in voluminous costume
jewels and shrill polyesters—
                        ambitious as a moth
to mime the dangerous leaf on which she rests.

PART THREE
FROM *COASTLINES* (1992)

To the memory of my mother

Virginia H. Ormsby

I
A FLORIDA CHILDHOOD

Le inutili macerie del tuo abisso
—Eugenio Montale, *Ossi di seppia*

MY FIRST BEACH

It used to say *No Picnicking* in three
languages: in English and in Spanish and
in Yiddish. The Yiddish looked
spidery and mysterious. And on
the frond-green benches, in a
precious shade, fixed-income pensioners
from Jersey or Connecticut would chat
and snooze. (Their poverty was hidden,
but I'd heard grown-up anecdotes of
skimpy suppers and of scavenging.)

Beyond their benches was the wall, a low
and plump-stoned wall of coral rock.
To me it meant that here the beach began.
Dim, indecisive waves lay just ahead.
Here there were picnics, here the tanned
paraded, muscular with oil, though now and then
you could spot pale newcomers with their
cuffs and collars still
stenciled on their unsunned skin.
I walked backward to anticipate
the waves of my first beach, which I could hear
sloshing behind me till they sounded like
the soapy buckets supers scattered down
Manhattan stoops, or tarpaulins upended
with taut rain. I walked backward out of
loyalty to those old people whom I'd had to pass
before the seawall, as though by privilege
I owed them cognizance till out of sight.

But here, before the open waves, where beach
umbrellas bloomed in tulip rows, I had
the feeling that comes on you in a dream
of moving through some unfamiliar house
in August when the rooms are full of sun
and past each open doorway you can glimpse
still further doorways brightened by a light
that has the spectral texture of your sleep,
is generous and almost palpable,
and even has a fragrance of its own,
warm and brightly drowsy, vanishing.

That was the dreamy feeling of my beach
that didn't last. For there I saw
the white-ribbed wavelets bundle to the shore,
like old men emptying their pockets out,
objects turned and smoothed for use,
if we still knew to use them, not
only sea bottles darkened by the sun,
lost combs with swirls of seaweed in their teeth,
bones and obvious corals, brachiated
candlesticks of sponge and snarls of line,
but what I still could just identify:

tar nuggets, terrible twists of wood, the arms of stars.

REMEMBRANCE
For Bruce Rickenbacher

In dream sometimes there is the glamour of
an animal but, afterwards,
alphabets emerge and people learn the monikers
reserved from all eternity for things.
The children are in love with etiquettes
and smell the sap inside the winter trees.
Old knuckles whiten on suspended porches.
You have the sense of sunlight where there move
figures of recollection wearing aprons and
a pair of vocal earrings, click of house shoes,
the comfort of a long-anticipated sigh.

If only recollection could cohere! If only
memory were cogent once again!
The dispersed tatters of an ancient page
resume themselves in the curator's bath,
or an old text millennia-unread
borrows coherence in a scholar's head,
or as at nightfall once, above the Glades,
we witnessed ibises flap up and wheel
like scattered flecks of newsprint whipped by wind
that skim breeze-bellied on warm drafts of air,
a pandemonium of blank white wings,
spiky hysteria of hoots and swerves
that steadily assembled into unisons of
swoops and slow encirclings, the loveliness
a single and concerted curve assumes
when many turn, and turn again, as one,
and so remembrance gathers islands up
and stitches estuaries to the gulf.

HORSESHOE CRAB

She is surprising in her lowliness.
She follows the immemorial furrows
along the tidal floor of the bay.
Her manufactured look disarms,
brown as molded plastic or poured bronze.
The silt-dulled sheen of her carapace
fits the hand, despite thorny protrusions
of chitin and that lacerating icepick
of tail.
        Underneath her frail rigidity,
sculpted like the death mask of a queen,
her pale, segmented legs beckon and gleam.

ADAGES OF A GRANDMOTHER

Grandmother said to me, "Keep thyself
unspotted from the world." She spoke in quotes.
I got the feeling that she had rehearsed
all her admonitions as a child,
for when she issued them to me she grew
solemn and theatrical. I knew
she tasted in her words some sweet,
indissoluble flavor of the past; but even more,
as though at eighty-five or eighty-six,
she stood still in the parlor of her recitation—
a plain, studious girl with long brown braids
(I have the portraits of her as a child)—
and spoke her lessons for approving guests.
Such touches of girlishness accompanied
her adages. And then she gave me dimes
for so many lines of Shakespeare memorized.
For "The quality of mercy" I was paid
a quarter, and at tea I gave her guests
a dollar's worth of Shakespeare with their toast.
"All the world's a stage," she reminded me.

Only armed with an adage might I sally forth.
"A foolish son's his mother's grief," she thought.
The world was scriptural and stratified.
It held raw veins of wisdom in its side,
like the Appalachians when we journeyed north.
She sat in the front seat of the Buick, hair net drawn
over her white hair coiled in a dignified bun,
her straw beflowered hat alert and prim.
From the back seat I'd study her, my grim
grandmother, with her dictatorial
chin, her gold-rimmed spectacles ablaze with all
the glory of the common highway where
field daisies spoke to her in doctrinaire,
confidential accents of the master plan
confided to grandmothers by the Son of Man.

Wisdom was talismanic and opaque,
could be carried in a child's small fist
like the personal pebble I fished out of the lake.
And whenever I stepped outside she kissed
my head and armed me with a similitude.
Beyond the screen door, past the windowsill,
the bright earth rang with providence until
even the wise ants at my shoe tips moved
in dark amazements of exactitude,
and the small dusty sparrows swooped innumerably.

I write this on the sunporch of the house
where she lay, an invalid, in her last years.
And I'm abashed to realize I blamed
her stiffness and her stubborn uprightness
for much that happened to me afterward.
Now I look through the window where she looked
and see the sunlight on the windowsill
and wonder what it signifies,
for now I barely recognize
her world outside, as though sunlight effaced
not only human features but their memory.
Her adages are all scattered in my head
(*Neither a borrower nor a lender be*)
and I cannot think for thinking of the dead
(*Go to the ant, thou sluggard,*
consider her ways, and be wise).
I cannot read the world now with her eyes.
I, who used to blame her so,
rummage in my pockets for
a nickel's worth of wisdom for my kids.

GRACKLE

It's hard not to like the wise-
guy grin, the almost sarcastic chatter
of the boat-tailed grackle by the Everglades
Cafe. He has an acrid cackle,
a cacophony of slick and klaxon cries,
with tinsel whispers like a breathy flute.
His repertoire seems meant to flatter
us by mimicry and so exonerate
our grosser faults, our greeds,
our clumsy cunnings, our minute
duplicities.
                Watch how he hops elastically
from roof beam down to a potato chip
and shrills and wheedles while his hard claws grip
whittled bench rims and the slats of rails.
He strides like a chimney sweep,
char-colored, and yet, see:
his cinder eyes are absolute.
Cunning of hunger makes his feathers bright
in smoky lapis, iris-indigo.

A FLORIDA CHILDHOOD

The brick-red Spanish roof tiles overlapped in patterns
reminiscent of a snake's scales, and the rain spouts held
emaciated fingers to the soaking eaves. The windows
flickered eyelids with oblique
pupils of lamplight muffled beyond the glass.
Some houses were grandees. Others wore
palm fringes at their throats like swaddled
muftis whose senescent eyes
fluoresced like aggies. At the banyan's thunderous
foot we gambled on mumblety-peg. I saw
spiders blazing coldly like far-off stars
while the pink dewdrops wobbled on their webs.
An ancient scorpion dwelt behind the broom.
Its warm brown eyes gazed in two rows from the tip
of its head like the curtained windows of a ship.
Its immobility made me dream of voyages.
And the blue-muscled skinks along the pebbles
sported tuxedo twills down their deceptive backs.
There I pierced a grasshopper with a sharpened match
and once, in a solution hole
of the hammock, I bellied deep into the moist
limestone crevices of a decaying reef. The earth
smelled fresh as a new-worn shoe. I could have
dozed forever in that unmarked place. The soft
desperate moths at nightfall sealed our house,
and the thresholds were spelled. Only the brass
hours chimed from the London clock, and the moon
grappled in its white branches at the windowsill.

LIVE OAK, WITH BROMELIADS

The live oak tufted with bromeliads
by the salt lagoon looks almost scarred.
Air plants bristle on its gray
limbs like knotted sprigs of surgeon's thread.
In sprawling notches of the canopy
Spanish moss dangles in snarled clusters,
while the long sunshine of Miami's winter
lends it a gloss of fractured malachite.

But nothing could be less wounded than this oak.
Its knuckled roots infiltrate the dank
marsh of the hammock, they drink the sand
riddled by land crabs to a moon-pocked surface.
And look:
                    like praying candles in a smoky shrine
set up to honor the salt god of the marsh,
the ranked branches embrace their parasites.

FRAGRANCES

The threshold of your mother's room had such
intimate possession of itself, and that
satin fabric that the lamp assumed
among the vanities, the combs and pins . . .
complexities of being soft and cool,
intricacy of clothing, lace and tulle,
the look of the half-shut chiffonier
with all the lank, soft-folded garments there;
the colors of her things in the dim lamp—
almost unsayable, that gentian sleeve.

And sometimes I would hide in her wardrobe,
standing among the dresses and the gowns
as though a rush of women circled me
with a smell of warm and fragrant skin
mingled with lilac and the blush of sun,
just as the golden sunshade made a glow
in which we all looked suddenly transformed,
illumined in the fragrance of the sun
that had a tinge of everlastingness,
the way verbena lingers on the tips
of all your fingers when you say goodbye.

FLORIDA BAY

A flittering of breeze, so hesitant,
rustles my face before the sun is up,
so subtle that it seems the diffident
touch of my children's fingers on my cheek.
I sit there with a wobbly coffee cup
cocked on one drowsy knee. For over a week
this tender predawn breeze has signaled day.
It blows here from the south, from Florida Bay,

where Florida curves westward to the Gulf,
the continent's dead end, our Finistère.
If you turn inward now to find yourself
as you once were, you will ignore that breeze
with its humid scent of flowers. There,
in the brightening room, old recollections tease
and elude you in forgotten things
while morning flickers with premonitory wings.

I used to wonder why I felt so out,
not seeing that it was my mulish nature.
And now, at fifty, when I've just about
finished with childhood (though dissatisfied),
the child's desolation, his nomenclature
of loneliness, projected and identified
with the furniture of Sunday dining rooms
after the pot roast and the macaroons,

still so possesses me.
                    And though we leave
the darkness of their tears behind the door,
shut our ears to their cries, refuse to grieve
for those we hated with the force of love,
their desperation not to be forgotten or
forsaken follows us till we are victims of
every laceration of their breath
that will not leave us even in their death.

And desolation will always be those warm
Miami afternoons when August rain
accumulated in the distance, before the storm
amassed and broke, and plump drops lashed
the tattered fronds outside, or hurricane
roared from Tortugas north with stillness stashed
inside its eye, and we waited for the wind
to flay the stucco and leave the banyan skinned.

Waiting, waiting—childhood solitude
of toys in the moted morning sun—
O intimations of a requiem. The mood
befell me like the sweet metallic tune
of a Sunday carousel before the ride is done,
that sense of perpetual and soon-
to-be-cherished happiness. . . . Remember your surprise
at the candled mirrors that returned your eyes

in diamond encirclings till you'd spot
an icicle kaleidoscope of yourself
amid the ponies' melodious trot,
and think, Is *that* me? Is *that* my face?
as though a stranger lent you a strange self
that stared back at you from the secret place
mirrors rise out of, or the near-familiar look
of photos of cousins tucked in an old schoolbook.

Remember the smell of the hall bookcase?
Inside the little mullioned panes that held
embrittled paperbacks, you saw your face
compromised by shadows and were scared,
while with a smudging fingerprint you spelled
the titles of the books in French or stared
at foxed engravings in the *Illustrated
London News*, its fashions of the celebrated

looking so weird in the Miami light,
the roach specks and the spider silk impressed
with long-squashed rosebuds in a tome clapped tight
for decades. And dead Cousin Arthur's photograph,
his First Communion suit, his parents dressed
in ascots and in flounces, a pleased faint laugh
beginning at the corners of his mouth,
among shrill memorabilia of the South:

taffeta bows, a dance card, a leather purse
embossed *Havana*, steamship souvenirs,
pearl opera glasses, scraps of verse
in coffee-colored copperplate, a lock of hair,
child's hair, beribboned, and the quaint gold shears
that snipped it, in a reticule. Aware
even then of the poisons of the past,
you touched these keepsakes warily at the last.

Is this where desolation began?
In that artifice of intimacy
I suffered then? I was the "little man,"
the fragile simulacrum of the male
swaddled in fisticuffs and mock gentility.
I puffed a self out on the sail
of my matchbox boat that skimmed the pond,
its makeshift mainstay bowing as it swanned.

You'll know mementos by their bandages,
their plush and tissue gauzes: *safe from life*!
They are embowered like the unopened pages
in those old volumes you would puzzle over,
their signatures uncut by the curious knife
and only dreamy fade marks on the cover.
But in the end I'll pack the books away
and go outside, drive south, toward Florida Bay

where the peninsula, above the Keys,
opens into an unimpeded view.
There once I saw the white birds from their rookeries
of bobbing islands clatter up and fly
and though I cling to memory, as if I knew
devotion were fiercer than that wing-divided sky,
I'll bow before them as they skim the ground:
outside ourselves is where our selves are found.

II
THE WAY NORTH

And mossy scabs of the wormfence, and heaped stones, and elder and mullen and pokeweed.

—Walt Whitman, "Song of Myself"

HIGHWAY GRASSES

The subtle undulations of the grass
along the highway held the shape of the wind.
The grass blades stooped like fragile flames
of candles ruffled by a child's
puffed breath, then seemed to cower down,
enfolded their stalks with neighbor stalks
in a seethe of symmetry.
                              The roadside grasses
tossed back while the wind defined itself
against their festive tassels, and their unison
moved me more than the delicate
nugget colors of their swaying stems
or the breathing bunches of sound
their tops together gave, like
conversations carried by the wind
in a language you can hear but not
make meaning of.
                      The pleasure of the tall
October grasses on the highway to the south
rippled along their simultaneous
stalks the way affectionate laughter
moves the guests to lean across the table
closer to each other, momentaneous
communities.

SAVANNAHS

Here the statues turn to fountains, here cascades
commandeer the dreams of roustabouts, here
smokestacks have a sheen of abnegation, and
the mortifying pleasures of the pool
nuzzle our nerve ends with their premonitions of
some luminance of bodies, of the flesh
made pure and whole beyond disdain, and we
acknowledge the savannahs of our origins,
those smooth, descending pastures to the sea,
as though the sea spelled freedom, or as though
its candor could awaken our dull eyes, as
though its bitter liberation on the tips of our
tongues announced some life resumed, some
pearl-embedded possible, some promise still
embowered, though only in the memories of words
do the lashed waters yip and congregate,
and rain along the violet skin of the waves
puckers like stings along a horse's hide.

I knew only the yearning of savannahs,
the delicate monotonies of grass stems
proffering some tasseled pagination of the wind,
and something of the exultation of
my knees, so long ago, the ecstatic
scars of elbows, gave me back
the pebble rainbows of the unloved ground.
There were no wings unequal to my heart then
and I sifted music through
the deft tendrils of my fingertips,
as though the heart were estuary to
the island-gathering, astringent sea.

MULLEIN

A pleasure secret and austere.
—Archibald Lampman, "In November"

1

Death is a kind of opportunity,
deprivation possibility,
where this weed sinks its root.
The mullein's infinitesimal black seeds
crave for vacancy to germinate.
It startles me to see it colonnade
defoliated roadsides and in June, impressed,
I round its plush and nettled obelisk.
From winter-clenched rosettes it pokes, man-high,
and grows big and green where other green things die.

All verticality, the mullein has a plumed,
columnar stature with upcurled
leaves that stand out from its stalk
like stiffened shavings on a whittled stick.
And from these curlicue-attentive leaves
the raceme of the mullein with
its padded shaft ascends, a quilted
polygon. And all along the raceme's
naked length, little flowers appear,
yellow-petaled to the pinnacle.

2

In vinyl bedrooms of cold-eyed hotels,
when I'm unable to imagine home
and when my own grim turn of mind
depopulates familiarity,
and nothing can people my sleep again,
I sometimes glimpse a mullein by the weed-
whacked border of the parking lot,
invisible though so conspicuous
beyond the stuttering whiteness of the flood-
lit asphalt, or poplaring a sewer pipe,

and I like the way, from what nobody else
would bother with, it sends a column up.
I like that it domesticates
small desolations and that it pinches place
from peripheries where places cannot be
and that its wispy petal sweetens haggardness.
I like out of how little mullein makes
a shade. So it can mollify the bleak
suite, the long hours of the night coming on,
that lurid doily with its Gideon.

3

If I were given to apostrophe,
I'd say to mullein, "Poke up, sprout, extend!
Be opportunistic, shrewd, exuberant.
Along storm gutters or the rims
of gaudy troughs of algae-ruffled seepage,
still be gauntly numerous, redeem the brink,
sentinel the emptiness seraphically.
Drive your root in nihil till it spout
and flutter out, to pleasure flies and bees,
your thin yellow flowers of astonishment."

CHILDHOOD HOUSE
For my brother Alan

After our mother died, her house, our
childhood house, disclosed
all its deterioration to our eyes.
While living she had screened us from, or we hadn't seen,
the termite-nibbled floorboards and the rotting beams;
the wounded stucco hidden by shrubbery; the frayed,
unpredictable wiring and the clanking labor
of the hot-water line into the discolored
tub; the fixtures in the dining room
skewed and malfunctioning.

                        I remember thinking with a
swarm of confusion that this was the true state
of our childhood now: this house of dilapidated girders
eaten away at the base. Somehow I had assumed
that the past stood still, in perfected effigies of itself,
and that what we had once possessed remained our possession
forever, and that at least the past, our past, our child-
hood, waited, always available, at the touch of a nerve,
did not deteriorate like the untended house of an
aging mother, but stood in pristine perfection, as in
our remembrance. I see that this isn't so, that
memory decays like the rest, is unstable in its essence,
flits, occludes, is variable, sidesteps, bleeds away, eludes
all recovery; worse, is not what it seemed once, alters
unfairly, is not the intact garden we remember but,
instead, speeds away from us backwards terrifically
until when we pause to touch that sun-remembered
wall, the stones are friable, crack and sift down,
and we could cry at the swiftness of that velocity
if our astonished eyes had time.

OLD PHOTOGRAPHS OF CHILDREN

The cracked and spotted photographs
of children dead a century before
pierce us when we look at them.
The glister of an eye
long consigned to cinders and
the maggot's mercies
engages our gaze.
How near these children seem to us
and yet how intimate with
nothingness, as though for them
the double kingdom lay
already open as a realm of light.
The sureties of hopefulness
burning in their long-dead look
disturb our own uncertainty, refuse
our knowledge of a future that awaits
beyond the borders of the photograph.
We have the superior sense
that we encompass these children in their ignorance
of all that happened since they left their pose,
unless we come to see how they elude
all our displaced solicitude,
their silver and palladium faces clasped
in the fragile grandeur of daguerrotypes.

GARTER SNAKE

The stately ripple of the garter snake
in sinuous procession through the grass
compelled my eye. It stopped and held its head
high above the lawn, and the delicate curve
of its slender body formed a letter S—
for "serpent," I presume, as though
diminutive majesty obliged embodiment.

The garter snake reminded me of those
cartouches where the figure of a snake
seems to suggest the presence of a god,
until more flickering than any god
the small snake gathered glidingly and slid,
but with such cadence to its rapt advance
that when it stopped once more to raise its head
it was stiller than the stillest mineral,
and when it moved again it moved the way
a curl of water slips along a stone
or like the ardent progress of a tear
till deeper still it gave the rubbled grass
and the dull hollows where its ripple ran
lithe scintillas of exuberance,
moving the way a chance felicity
silvers the whole attention of the mind.

OF PARADISE AS A GARDEN

For Ricardo Pau-Llosa

The symmetry of cycads with their fire-colored
cones and mandala-fringed fronds, the
precarious peace of epiphytes, orchids
with long-suffering corollas, the whiteness
of vanilla's petals and that scent. . . . And
there are here small advantageous vistas
where you glimpse across lagoons
the only infinities we're ready for,
that faded, hardly bluish edge of sky
with its reminiscent tint. Here the shade
of colonnades affords
presentiments of paradise, the lanes
not of some featureless peace
but of calm among spontaneous
freshets, exploratory orders that bemuse
the intellect, and a continual,
undisappointed hope, not as yearning but
anticipation, not hope as torment,
as it is in life, but all the pleasures
of fulfillment there, a longing that is
ever realized, the loveliness of the familiar,
the alphabet of friendship learned again,
not loneliness but only the garden's green,
where all the exiles find their homes again.

HALIFAX

Everyone enfolds a city so
cordoned from the ordinary, pinnacled
and musketed, with steeples
sleek in their stickling rectitude,
remote and rainy, on its point of sea,
with pomp of foghorns pulsing from the buoys.

Such inward cities have the radiant
tedium of childhood. There
the salt-scathed asphalt shone and the prim
crimson of the bandstand, in
the Public Gardens, echoed
November's roses. There the decorous
chrysanthemums inaugurated
avenues of rain.

These hidden cities have the homeliness
of Haligonian Sundays in the fall,
after the service, when the reverend
fumbled the sermon and the gawky choir
still thumped and trilled so woefully,
and all the heaviness of afternoon
poured down until the emblematic
windows of the saints
bared their antimonies:
All life is heaviness
in secret cities when November comes.

In Halifax the shrill ferry already
sloshes at the prompt piers. A seagull
on a scavenged bag
mewls into the saturated sky.
The cities of remembrance all are ports
where every sabbath of the autumn tolls and
even weeping seems gratuitous.

THE PUBLIC GARDENS

The Public Gardens are so cunningly
laid out. The boxwood has symmetrical
barbarity of shape. And the walkway
with its fractal jaggedness dissuades
the eye. Linden colonnades will shine
like faces at a solemn protocol
brushed with tears. In November, the long line
of the damp trees oppresses. The blades
of the tall grasses spiral sinuously.
There is a definitive edge to the border
of the hoed-up beds. This is a place of order,
despite its delicate wilderness disarray.

Here, three years ago, I watched a swan
trundle in a chicken-wire enclosure
like something perishable stored up for the spring.
The swan looked muddy and obese.
Its horny, latex-colored feet unnerved
me. This was not the virile, ominous
swan of Yeats, the gliding cynosure
of all imagination. Only a close-docked wing
remained of all that majesty. Beyond the wan,
superannuated roses, brambled and brown-edged,
full of some fear that I could taste, police
cars by the black gates wetly reconnoitered
where hunched, unshaven men smoked and loitered,
and the festive statues, rain- and mildew-ledged,
gestured spaciously with luminous

fingers where the civic soot collected.
The swan brought back to mind a horrible
thing I'd seen there once, a hungry seagull
perched upon a half-dead mallard's back
and eating its raked and squirming flesh alive.
It might have been hideously symbolical—
the mystical amalgam of two beasts
in which the stronger on the weaker feasts—
but for the pitiful, writhing, bony neck
of the injured duck. Its pain deflected
Darwinian pieties, too bland in any case to give
individual significance to pain,
and I remembered how, some weeks before,
I'd eaten roast duck with a rich plum sauce.
Here was the flesh itself, with crass
thrashings agonizing, while the quick gull tore
slivers of slitted skin and dabbled its bill again
in flinching meat.
                    Pain estranges,
cordons the sufferer and disarranges
pity in its strict perimeters:
I thought of people I'd known, sufferers
so perimetered by pain that only love
could touch them still—sometimes, not even love.

With a stick I chased away the gull above,
and then I laid the stick along the torn duck's neck
and leaned until it broke with a little click
and both its wings fanned out reflexively
tremoring and hovering and an almost terrible
exhilaration poured along my hands and arms,
though I felt also the nausea you feel
when pain intrudes on beauty and disarms
the order obligatory for the beautiful,
and I knew how much I'd loathed that hurt bird,
that had suffered so like me,
or you, in muddy miserable twitches, wincingly.

I left the Public Gardens with its rows
of neatly mattocked beds, I, a poet, one of those
virtuosos of the nerves, and what had I seen,
suppurative, shame-naked, and obscene?
In muted wards, some agony unwinds;
beyond the still facades, behind Venetian blinds,
some passion exacts its ritual
desecration of the actual.
The horror in my mouth was almost prayer,
the stumbled syllables of those in despair,
and yet, so poetical, so apposite!
Does order merely gauze the infinite
wince of the brided skin? And was pity
conferral of extinction or the first stone of the city
founded in love?
That day, I saw the fountains with their casual
music of refusal
splash beyond, while in its pen the great
mud-spattered swan beaked its black gate.

RAILWAY STANZAS

I have always found railway stations sad.
The aura of departure lingers there.
The rails that stretch away in parallel
abraded brightnesses dismay, like those problems
in your old mathematics book at school;
outmoded, they yet sting the intellect
with formalin conundrums of the time that's left.
I think of all the leavetakings I've known.
Airports are abstract. Railroads have
valedictory fragrances—the seethe of steam,
a scorched whiff of oil. I think of
lovers waving as the platform fades.

And yet, a hankering for depots, terminals,
is a symptom of good health, a robust mind.
Arrivals also figure in my dreams
where they take on the shape of engine spokes.
I used to see the spokes and wheels as a frieze,
not as an engine but a dark geometry,
tableaux of pistoned possibilities,
without a single ledge for tears,
without the ineluctable hankie of farewells,
the blurred mascara of a momma's eyes,
Dad's mustache all atremble, baby's howls,
the structure of forsakenness as the station speeds

out of sight and hearing into memory:
the dainty Edwardian melancholy
of junctions, switching places, water tanks;
the bright red afterthought of the caboose
with men, suspendered, sucking corncob pipes
on the little black-railed platform at the back;
and there was also the sleek smell of rails,
the bitter cloudiness of iron gauge,
the creosote-soaked ties and the gouging spikes,
the deferential signal bars, the throb of the shrill
light. But most, a pale opacity of windows
in a nighttime train, a glimpse of shaded lamps

and diners all embraced in goldenness
and wisps of smoke, the porter leaning between
the sleeper and the observation car—
watched in a shriek of speed from a trestle by
the slow, muddy river underneath.
And sometimes I had stuck a silver dime
to the outer rail before the train went by
and now retrieved it as the distance took
that companionable apocalypse away:
the coin was faceless now and hammered flat
and it felt hot and smooth and was transformed
in my fingers to a fossil of velocity.

I do not write this from nostalgia.
I who once revered as a mercy of
certitude the benignity of fact
am skeptical of every reverie
that leads me backward into dubious time.
A sense of destination, though, beguiles
me still, the piercing and metallic scent
of almost indiscernible adieux.
It is momentum now that holds me, the
quick kiss on the steps, the conductor's
cry, the stirring of the iron wheels
in spires of steam toward their unyielding speed.

GETTING READY FOR THE NIGHT

When Grandma combed her fine white hair at night
until it toppled to her shoulder blades
in startling cascades, bright-angel-winged,
she looked like Milton's angel at the gate
of paradise: sovereign, ingenuous, and stern.
I marveled in the ripples of her hair
the teasing and impertinent lamplight touched,
but "Won't you clip my toenails for me now?"
she said and then, with a stoic sigh,
"It's hard to be so old, so incapable."

I didn't want to touch her pallid foot,
and yet it felt astonishing when her left
foot nestled in my clasp and I began
scissoring the wrinkled horn of nail
with snipping shears until the pale
translucencies of toenail ribboned off.
Her sole felt warm in my deft paw
and suddenly I could appreciate
Grandma being mortal, one who sheds
skin and nails and all integuments.

                    But then she twined
and spooled her colorless flat hair
about accustomed fingers into supple
braids
              and I was baffled in the tenderness
her silk-shaded light winked down on both of us.

I snipped her toenails
evenly. Together we prepared her
for the night. Together we made sure
that, shorn and braided, she would enter into
the encirclements of darkness just beyond
the pooled, penurious
empire of the lamp.

NOVA SCOTIA

The topography is of slight relief, and innumerable lakes, streams, bogs, barrens, and stillwaters occur.

—Flora of Nova Scotia (*1945*)

For David Solway

Here, south of Halifax, near Peggy's Cove,
where the coastline shoulders out into the sea,
you search the landscape for its difficult
splendor. There are sudden gullies and domes
littered with glacial boulders in a jagged
equipoise. The glacier's nosing wedge
disheveled all the hillsides and the stones
seem sprinkled by a child. Gargantuan
spills of granite balance on dainty
hillocks and the mauve arroyos
have a stunned and smoky look
like gaping survivors of some detonation.

Each thing seems hieroglyphic to your eye.
Tough decumbencies of spurge
thicken the glance. The cheeks of rocks
are bearded with lichens in rough,
persistent whorls. Sometimes in a crevice
of the cast-up rock you'll come upon
improbable orchids, or a bullfrog croaks
from one of the many little pools of rain
skittered by windblown spray. Maybe you'll find
fragments of shell and glass that have
the cadence of the North Atlantic in their
sleek, barbaric shapes. But
the narrow pathway twists between
contiguous desolations, indifferent
to history, and there is
the momentary, quickly avoided sense
that all we cling to here is scaffolding
above slashed granite and the ocean's voice.

You won't sing hymns to seals
along the sharp immersions of this coast,
nor will you drink transfiguring
mouthfuls of the pure and bitter wind
from your chill, chapped hands.
But maybe there your moment will arrive
unaccompanied by memory
or expectation, and you'll see
simply what lies before you or ahead,
observe it with a purgatorial
precision of the eye,
and speak it in the justice of the tongue.

Later, beyond the coastline you will come
out of season to the dark hotel
where your room overlooks the sea.
The gaudy awnings will be rolled up for the spring,
the seaward patio swept bare, the hulls
of summer's pleasure boats aligned
and tarpaulined, and maybe there will be
a single lantern with its oily light
reflected in the ocean of November.
There in your seclusion from the wind
all night in dreams of home you'll listen for
the cold companionship of distant waves,
hear squalls beating and the seethe of foam.

Abstracted from particulars, alone
with the uncertain fluttering of your breath,
you'll listen to rafters creaking and the clack of glass
and in the far-off vehemence of that darkness, still
suspended between memory and hope,
all night you'll hear
the North Atlantic, just beyond the cove,
banging its knuckles on the heartless sill.

NOTES TO THE POEMS

"What It Is Like to Be a Bat" takes its title from an essay by the philosopher Thomas Nagel.

"A Crow at Morning" uses the Talmudic term *hefker,* which means "ownerless" or perhaps "up for grabs," as in money found lying in a street (see *Baba Meẓia*).

"Mutanabbi in Exile" paraphrases a famous verse by the real Mutanabbi in the final four lines (translated literally in the epigraph to the second section of Part One).

In "Mutanabbi Remembers His Father," the Arabic words given are meaningless mnemonic formulae used to denote specific prosodic meters; here the meter so designated is *kamil,* the "perfect" meter: ⌣⌣‒⌣‒ ⌣⌣‒⌣‒ ‒‒⌣‒.

"The Caliph" is based on details from the reign of the sixth Fatimid Caliph of Egypt, al-Hakim bi-Amr Allah, who ruled from 996 until his mysterious disappearance in 1021. For the facts of the poem, see the *Encyclopaedia of Islam* (new edition), vol. III, pp. 76–81. For "May God pray for them!"—which plays on the pious formula traditionally applied to the Prophet Muhammad—see S. D. Goitein, *Studies in Islamic History and Institutions* (Leiden: E. J. Brill, 1968), especially p. 78: "Since prayer is the most significant occupation of the pious, it is unimaginable that God should not pray himself."

"Finding a Portrait of the Rugby Colonists" refers to the utopian community founded by Thomas Hughes in 1881 in Rugby, Tennessee, north of Knoxville, where my grandmother and her sisters grew up.

ACKNOWLEDGMENTS

My thanks to the editors of these journals, in which versions of poems have appeared:

America: "December"

The Antigonish Review: "Starfish"

Blueline: "The Gossip of the Fire," "Highway Grasses," "History," "Mullein," "An Oak Skinned by Lightning," "Railway Stanzas," "Railyard in Winter," "River Plants," "Spider Silk," "Wood Fungus"

The Boston Review: "Gravediggers' April"

Descant: "Baudelaire to Mme. Aupick," "Fragrances," "Hate," "Of Paradise as a Garden"

Double Take: "Blood"

The Fiddlehead: "Rooster"

The Gettysburg Review: "A Crow at Morning," "Flamingos"

Grand Street: "Mutanabbi in Exile"

Index: "Gazing at Waves"

Mockingbird: "Amber," "Nova Scotia" (excerpt)

The New Republic: "Anhinga," "Fragrances," "Origins," "The Suitors of My Grandmother's Youth"

The New Yorker: "Adages of a Grandmother," "The Ant Lion," "The Caliph," "Childhood House," "Conch Shell," "Fingernails," "For a Modest God," "Garter Snake," "Getting Ready for the Night," "Grackle," "My Mother in Old Age," "Rain in Childhood"

The Other Side: "Skunk Cabbage"

The Oxford American: "Finding a Portrait of the Rugby Colonists"

The Paris Review: "Mutanabbi Praises the Prince"

Poetry Wales: "Mutanabbi Remembers His Father"

Pulpsmith: "Quark Fog"

The Quarterly: "Crab," "Foundry," "Lazarus in Skins," "Lichens," "Moths at Nightfall," "Spider"

Salmagundi: "What It Is Like to Be a Bat"

Shenandoah: "Forgetful Lazarus," "Lazarus and Basements," "Lazarus in Sumatra," "Lazarus Listens"

The Southern Review: "Florida Bay," "Hand-painted China"

Southwest Review: "Nose"

The Toronto Star: "Old Photographs of Children"

Wilderness: "Horseshoe Crab"

"Origins," "Skunk Cabbage," and "Starfish" have been anthologized in *The Norton Anthology of Poetry* (4th ed.; New York: Norton, 1996). "My Mother in Old Age" was anthologized in *The Norton Introduction to Literature* (5th ed.; New York: Norton, 1991). "Bavarian Shrine" received special commendation in the 1985 Arvon International Poetry Competition and appeared in the Arvon *Anthology* in 1987. "Adages of a Grandmother" will appear in *Literature: The Human Experience* (7th ed.; New York: St. Martin's Press, 1997). "Rooster" has been anthologized in *Fiddlehead Gold: Fifty Years of the Fiddlehead Magazine* (Fredericton, New Brunswick: The Fiddlehead, 1995). "Of Paradise as a Garden" appeared also in *Descant Chapbook: A Sampler* (Toronto: Descant, 1995).

"Childhood House," "Mullein" and "Statues and Mannequins" were translated into Czech by Hana Žantovská and broadcast in Prague in October 1992. Earlier versions of "What It Is Like to Be a Bat" and "Flamingos" appeared in *Acumen* and *Index*, respectively.

The poems in Parts Two and Three appeared first in book form in *Bavarian Shrine and Other Poems* (Toronto: ECW Press, 1990) and *Coastlines* (Toronto: ECW Press, 1992). I thank Robert Lecker of ECW Press for permission to reprint poems from these two collections as well as for his constant support of my work.

I am grateful to the Ingram Merrill Foundation for an award that gave me support and encouragement during the writing of many of these poems.

I wish to express special thanks to Alice Quinn for her constant strong support. I am also grateful to George Bradley for advice and much encouragement during the preparation of the present collection.